If it makes me feel bette why should I stop?

"Just leave me alone" or "What I need now is chocolate!" We've all said it, and most of the time it's not a problem at all.

But when you're feeling down, the things that get you through can also become the things that mess you up.

Being alone ends up isolating us. One bar of chocolate becomes a comfort eating habit. One drink becomes a whole bottle. One scratch becomes a cycle of risky self-harm. One question "Are you still my friend?" becomes a constant need for reassurance.

And instead of getting better, you get worse.

But this doesn't need to happen! Turn the page and you'll be taking the first step towards getting in control of the things you do.

3

YOU'RE ON YOUR WAY!

The first step is the most important

And you just took it. You made the decision to stop letting unhelpful behaviours mess up your life.

Now, we're going to help you work out what you're doing too much of, and then show you a simple 4-step way to stop or cut down.

How do you know when something is messing you up?

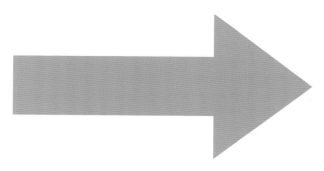

TURN OVER

IT AIN'T WHAT YOU DO, IT'S HOW MUCH YOU DO IT

We're not here to be killjoys. There's nothing wrong with chocolate, spending some time alone, or a bit of retail therapy.

But when you're feeling low, you can start to lean on these things, using them to help get you through a bad time.

Other, not so obvious behaviours can also be 'props'. Like hitting out at people – physically or just by shouting. Hurting yourself in different ways. Hiding away from the world.

Trouble is, too much of this kind of stuff makes you worse, not better. You get into a kind of vicious circle, doing something that seems to help for a bit, but finding that it actually makes life worse in the long run.

ARE YOU DOING TOO MUCH OF SOMETHING?

DRINKING	2 or 3 drinks a week	More than 2 or 3 a week but not getting drunk
EATING FOR COMFORT	Eating chocolate etc. occasionally	Eating a little when you feel upset
SPENDING TOO MUCH	Buying some things you just fancy	Buying some things that stretch you
TAKING RISKS	Seeing occasional risks as fun	You start to "up the stakes" to more dangerous risks
COMPLAINING	You say clearly what you feel and need	You moan a lot that "It's not fair"
BEING CLINGY	You lack some confidence at times	You want others to make important decisions for yo
HITTING OUT AT PEOPLE	You're sometimes rude when frustrated	You begin to throw your weight around
GOSSIPING	You tell others good news about your friends	You discuss good news told in confidence
SHOPLIFTING	Your friends say they shoplift and you don't tell them it's wrong	You're with friends when they steal and don't say anything
HIDING AWAY	You tend to be quiet in conversations	You avoid spending time with people

rink every day, netimes getting drunk	Getting really drunk when you're down	Getting drunk every day
:ing a lot when you feel set	Bingeing on food when you're upset	Bingeing and making yourself sick when you're upset
tting into debt – but der control	Spending far more than comes in each week – ignoring the consequences	Run out of credit, paralysed and overwhelmed by debt
I start to get minor ries	You do things that would put you in hospital if they went wrong	You do things that could be fatal for you or others
I get really upset if you n't get your own way	You get really worked up and upset others too	You are so upset you don't get on with other things and fall out with everyone
I ask other people's nions all the time	You need others to be near you to feel okay	Your confidence is shot - you can't face anything alone
I often hurt people you n't like	You hit out at people you love when you feel frustrated	You get into fights often - hurting people and being injured yourself
I love to discuss ople's private secrets	You get a reputation as someone who can't be trusted	No-one trusts you and you feel lonely
I take something small I say "it's no big deal"	You steal bigger and bigger things more and more often	Your shop-lifting continues and you start to steal in other ways too
I cross the road to id chats with people I know	You lose confidence and find it hard even knowing where to start a conversation	You stay in all the time feeling anxious, panicky and depressed

TURN

OK.
SO YOU
NEED TO
WORK ON
SOMETHING

Here's how…

First, don't beat yourself up. Most people get into a cycle of doing unhelpful things when they're feeling down.

The fact that you're reading this means you're on the way to fixing it.

All you have to do is choose one problem behaviour to work on, and follow our Easy 4-Step Plan (E4SP for short) to get control.

FIRST CHOOSE A PROBLEM

THE THINGS YOU DO

CHECKLIST - **SHEET 1**

ARE YOU

		TICK
DRINKING TOO MUCH	To improve how you feel - or improve how you sleep	
EATING FOR COMFORT?	It's called 'comfort eating'	
SPENDING TOO MUCH	It's called 'retail therapy'	
TAKING RISKS	You can cause yourself real damage	
SELF-HARM	It doesn't help for long	
BEING CLINGY	It pushes people away	
HITTING OUT AT PEOPLE	It can leave you feeling so alone	
BULLYING	It's not really strong	
SHOP-LIFTING	It's not too exciting getting a criminal record	
HIDING AWAY	Spirals down so you lose more & more confidence	

THAT MESS YOU UP

CHECKLIST – **SHEET 2**

ARE YOU

		TICK
BEING IMPULSIVE ABOUT IMPORTANT THINGS	e.g. resigning a job without really thinking it through	
SETTING YOURSELF UP TO FAIL / BE REJECTED	Doing things that prove you are bad, useless or a failure	
BECOMING A TV / INTERNET ADDICT	It's no substitute for real relationships	
WANTING OTHERS TO SORT OUT EVERY PROBLEM	It saps your confidence	
DOING, DOING, DOING	You've no time for your own needs	
DRINKING TOO MUCH COFFEE / COLA TO PERK YOURSELF UP	It messes up your sleep	
SLEEPING IN AND NAPPING THROUGH THE DAY	You won't sleep well at night	
PUTTING THINGS OFF	Frustrating for you and others	
WORRYING ALL THE TIME	Things go round and round but problems don't get sorted	

OTHER: PLEASE WRITE ANY OTHER THINGS YOU DO THAT MESS YOU UP HERE:

THIS WAY TO SOMETHING GOOD

NOW CHOOSE SOMETHING TO DO THAT HELPS

Choose a
sensible response

Just one tiny change to what you do and
how you react can make all the difference.

Like what?

Well, how about planning and preparing
for a good night's sleep. Or why not try
doing something that gives you a boost,
such as a hobby, having a relaxing bath, or
listening to music? Pick something that
you think you might feel motivated to do,
and of course something that you think
you could keep working at.

There are many helpful things that you
could do. Choose one or more that you
might do instead of the things you do that
mess you up.

**HELPFUL THINGS
CHECKLIST AHEAD!**

THE THINGS YOU

ARE YOU

		Tick
EATING REGULARLY AND HEALTHILY	Taking time to enjoy the food	
GIVING YOURSELF TIME TO SLEEP	It's a good start to any day	
KEEPING UP WITH ROUTINE THINGS	Ironing, housework, gardening	
DOING THINGS WITH OTHER PEOPLE	Spending times with family & friends, or by phone / letter / e-mail	
DOING THINGS THAT GIVE YOU A BOOST	e.g. hobbies, listening to music, having a nice bath that give you fun / pleasure	
SHARING PROBLEMS WITH TRUSTED FRIENDS & FAMILY	It can really help	
FINDING OUT MORE ABOUT HOW YOU FEEL	For example: attending a voluntary sector self-help group	
LIVING IN LINE WITH YOUR VALUES/IDEALS	Remember who you want to be	

DO THAT HELP

CHECKLIST - **SHEET 2**

ARE YOU

		Tick
FACING YOUR FEARS	Using slow steady steps	
DOING EXERCISE / GOING FOR WALKS / SWIMMING ETC.	It can give you a boost	
USING YOUR SENSE OF HUMOUR TO COPE	Laughter always helps	
PLANNING TIME FOR YOU AS WELL AS FOR OTHERS	Not giving all the time	
TAKING ANY PRESCRIBED MEDICINE REGULARLY	It can be part of the recovery process	
RELAXING/ BUILD IN GAPS IN THE DAY	Time for you. Music, reading, a bath - whatever works for you	
USING PEOPLE AROUND YOU	Your practitioner, family or friends - get them all on the job	
DOING THE ESSENTIALS	Don't let unpaid bills build up	

Q: AM I DOING OTHER THINGS
THAT HELP?
WRITE IN WHAT YOU ARE DOING
IF THIS APPLIES TO YOU

E4SP THIS WAY →

Break the problem into pieces

It's hard to stop doing something all at once, especially if you've been doing for ages, so break it into easy chunks.

So, if you've lost your confidence and are hiding away from the world, what could you do? You could break the week into bits and decide to do something with someone else on Mondays, for example.

Don't try and become a party animal yet - just work on a little bit of the problem - like getting out of the house.

Or if you're spending too much, start by just cutting out online shopping.

Most problems can be chopped up like this, and you're much more likely to succeed when you do things bit by bit.

Brainstorm ways to do the first piece

Grab a piece of paper and write down all the things you could do to work on the first bit of the problem.

To meet up with somebody on Mondays, for example, you could ask a friend round, meet one or more people somewhere quiet and comfortable, or try something small like an email, phone call or text. Do anything that reconnects you to others and moves things on.

The trick is to be creative and let your mind go. Write everything down - the ridiculous things as well as the sensible ones.

Do this and there's bound to be a good idea in there somewhere.

TURN OVER FOR STEPS 3 & 4

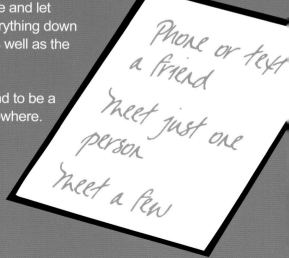

Choose an idea and make a plan to do it

Look at your list of ideas and pick one that looks do-able. Remember, to make a big change in your life you are best chunking this into a series of smaller pieces. Make sure that the steps are small, straightforward and seem like things you could really do.

Choose something that is:

- Useful for understanding or changing how you are
- Specific, so that you will know when you have done it
- Realistic, practical and achievable.

Make each step as small as you like.

Now plan out what you'll do and when.

- What are you going to do?
- When are you going to do it?

Make sure your plan doesn't push you too far or too fast. Make it slow and easy to do so you move forward step by step.

Going to meet on Monday? You need to get it sorted a day or so before. On the Saturday, text your friend and ask them round on Monday evening. Ask them to let you know if they can make it, or whether another time is better.

What if something gets in the way?

As soon as you've written your plan, think about what could stop it happening. Is there anything that might trip you up?

- What could arise, and how can you overcome any problems?

When you know what could block your progress, make a mini-plan for getting round the block.

This way, you'll be ready for whatever happens!

Check the plan and put it into action

This is it! You've made your plan, now you need to check that it's do-able. Use this checklist:

Is it realistic?
You're not planning to run a marathon are you?

Are you aiming at just one thing?
Don't try and do more than one item on your list. You can always pick another when you've sorted the first one.

Is it slow?
There's no need to rush at things. Your plan can take as long as you like, so long as you stick to it, step by step.

Is it easy?
Make your steps small and easy and you'll be more likely to do them.

Are you ready to unblock it?
Have you thought about what could go wrong and how to deal with it?

FIVE TICKS?

THEN GO FOR IT!

NOW
KEEP
IT
GOING!

Just take it step by step

Even a problem that seems huge can be tackled with the E4SP. The secret is breaking everything down into small, manageable pieces.

When you're making your plan, be sure that the steps are small and do-able. Plan to cut down unhelpful behaviours and replace them with helpful one's.

When you're doing your plan, take it step by step and if things get scary in the middle, give yourself a rest or a breather. If it seems too much- take a step back and do something a bit easier for a time.

Then get back on track, until you've put your plan into action.

Be steady and determined, use the E4SP and you will be able to stop doing the things that mess you up, and build more helpful responses.

Use the Planner sheet on pages 24/25 to help you plan these changes.

GOOD LUCK!

DON'T JUST SIT THERE, MAKE A PLAN!

1. WHAT AM I GOING TO DO?

2. WHEN AM I GOING TO DO IT?

3. WHAT PROBLEMS OR DIFFICULTIES COULD ARISE, AND HOW CAN I OVERCOME THEM?

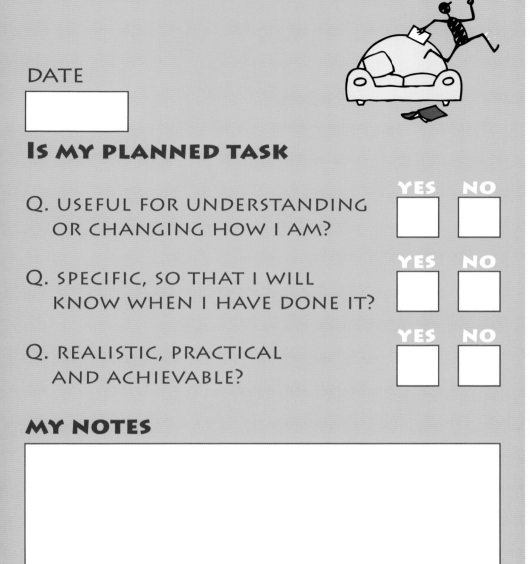

DATE

IS MY PLANNED TASK

Q. USEFUL FOR UNDERSTANDING
   OR CHANGING HOW I AM?

YES ☐ NO ☐

Q. SPECIFIC, SO THAT I WILL
   KNOW WHEN I HAVE DONE IT?

YES ☐ NO ☐

Q. REALISTIC, PRACTICAL
   AND ACHIEVABLE?

YES ☐ NO ☐

MY NOTES

PLEASE NOTE: If you are struggling or feel worse, or if at any time you feel suicidal please visit your doctor, attend A+E/the Emergency room, or phone the Samaritans, 111 or 999 (UK only)

WHERE TO GET EVEN MORE HELP

The E4SP works really well and if you need more detail (plus a lot more examples) get hold of 'How to Fix Almost Everything' - another booklet in this series.

But if you've tried the plan and come up against something you just can't seem to plan your way out of, you may need a bit more help than this little book can give. You can get added help and support by working through the free linked online modules at www.llttf.com.

When you've sorted your current problem, you might want to choose another little book and work on something else in your life. Here are some more little books that can help you deal with these things and start to feel better.

GOOD LUCK